WHAT THE WIND TAUGHT ME

Poems by
Pearl Werbach

BLUE LIGHT PRESS ◆ 1ST WORLD PUBLISHING

1st WORLD
PUBLISHING

SAN FRANCISCO ◆ FAIRFIELD ◆ DELHI

WHAT THE WIND TAUGHT ME

1ST WORLD LIBRARY
PO Box 2211
Fairfield, Iowa 52556
www.1stworldpublishing.com

BLUE LIGHT PRESS
www.bluelightpress.com
Email: bluelightpress@aol.com

BOOK, COVER DESIGN
Melanie Gendron

COVER ART
Copyright © Clare Rojas. All rights reserved

COVER CONCEPT
Lyn Werbach

AUTHOR PHOTO
Lyn Werbach

FIRST EDITION

Library of Congress Control Number: 2017951797

ISBN 9781421837826

To Papa,

Rest in peace.

CONTENTS

WHAT THE WIND TAUGHT ME

Why is the Moon Round?

The wind is loud because
if it weren't, it would have no trace of existence.
The moon is round so that
it has a face to smile with.
Besides, the aliens thought it looked better that way.
The trees sway because they are waving hello.
The birds fly because walking was too easy.
Books speak because
you read them with such curiosity.
The owl sings because
it wants to comfort the sky.
The marker writes because
without ink, it is just a piece of nothing.
The fire dances because
it is being tickled by the wind.
The zebra runs because
the savannah looks better with a smudge
of black and white.

What the Wind Taught Me

Let the grass mess up my hair
and the wind blow it back.
I am melted on the ground.
Alone, just me and the crows.
Alone, just me and the grass.
Alone, just me and the wind.

Maybe I am not alone.
The creak of the old cypress tree
sways over my eyes.
The wind is whispering an old secret from Asia
and a new one from South America.

Here's the secret:
I wasn't always just the wind.

Tossing the Moonlight

The mist puddled on the sidewalk
and greeted my tongue.
It watered the wilted plants
and crept silently
onto the roofs of sleeping houses.
The moon flashed cold, bright eyes
at the mist.
The mist tossed the light back up,
reflecting on and on,
like two mirrors
staring at each other.
They played this game until
the sun pushed the moon
out of the sky.

"Again, tonight!"
the moon whispered.

Ars Poetica

A poem is the rattling pipe in the basement
that keeps you awake.
A poem is a blooming flower,
opening only when the sun comes up.
A poem is an owl, gathering twigs for its nest.
A poem is a black pen, leaving a purple mark.
A poem is inspiration, ready to strike.
A poem is a mismatched floor tile.
A poem is the glittering moon
that just winked at me.
A poem is a passed-away friend
finding a new form of life.

The Next Blue Moon

The man on the moon winked at me!
I saw his reflection in the water,
under the shade of a tree.
He told me I was amazing and great.
He looked like a smiling plate.
The plate had faded grapes as craters,
blueberries as eyes,
and a banana as his smiling mouth.

Oh, how the next blue moon will shine!
How perfectly its craters will swim in white.
How young the man on the moon will seem.
It's all so amazing;
it almost feels like a dream.

Rainbow of the Night

The rainbow of the night,
shining stained glass in the sky
like a graceful fish moving its tail
side to side to side to side.
A painting unworthy of paper,
an idea jumping with vibrant colors.
An invention that does more
than what it's supposed to do.
The awe slipping out of my mouth,
taking form and color and movement of its own.
The northern lights, the rainbow of the night.

At Midnight

The photograph was smeared
with the years that had passed.
The man seemed older
than he was yesterday.
He was perched on a horse
with a midnight black coat of fur.
I squinted hard.
I could see stars in that midnight sky.
A battered cowboy hat
managed to fit on his head.
He smiled as he shook hands
with an old oak tree.

Only Me

Standing taller than the sky
with patterns more complex
than the bark of a tree,
I shine brighter than the sun,
but I am still only me.

Long, Rough Branches

Rustle rustle the tree said.
The wind had forced the words
out of the tree's worn out leaves.
It shook, trying to scare the wind away.
Finally, the wind fled.
The tree held its branches high in its triumph.
Regrowing new bark where the rain had bruised,
it healed quickly.
Opening its branches wide,
the squirrels and birds were invited back
to nest and rest
in the shadows of the tree.

Ode to the Rain

Clip, clap and another hollow sound.
It trembles the clouds
until they clatter and pound,
shooting arrows made of light.
Rain soaks the meadows
and fills the gutters,
hiding the sun from sight.
The clouds' cheeks, grey with fury,
snap the limbs of a tree,
but only until the sun smiles brightly again,
warming the air and erasing the sky.

Fallen Friend

For Lila, the blue parakeet

We will meet again,
I'm sure of it.
I'll spend my nights thinking of you,
in the time when I can't dream.
In a crowd,
my eyes and words will search,
for we will meet eyes again.

In the trees, I'll search.
In the breeze,
I'll listen
for your soft voice
or your chirping laugh.

And when I meet someone new,
I'll be thinking of you,
for we will meet again
once you come back.

Secrets of Animals

A dragonfly is a colorful, delicate buzz of a set of wings.
A hummingbird is a moving rainbow of music.
A robin is the red and brown welcome of spring.
A wolf is like a sudden whip of gray smoke,
hovering over a warm fire.
A dog is the lick of a soft tongue.
A cat is a furry, acrobatic pair of four legs.
A lion is a roar of fur.
A ladybug is like a unique piece of art
that cannot be framed.
A mouse is more than the hole in the wall
it climbs through.
An elephant is like an old chair
with big ears.
A zebra is a hoofed, black and white streak
over the golden, swaying fields.
A human being is a confused puzzle,
making things seem harder than they are.
A monkey is another spoken word,
but really, a speech of wonder.
A butterfly is the glittering stars
that you looked up at last night.

Another Reflection

Staring back at me,
doing what I do,
mimicking my thoughts and me.

With no voice or personality
of your own,
you copy an image of someone
or something.

Once they are out of sight,
you target something new.
Perhaps a toothbrush or a towel,
whatever you think is pretty.

Maybe next time,
you will have a face of your own,
with eyes and a personality.

The Angel's Call

I was about to close my eyes.
"When?" It asked, whispering,
as quiet as an owl's wings.
"Where?" It blew again.
"What, when, where, why?"
The wind shifted anonymously.
Suddenly, the wind became quiet,
and my sight no longer blurred.
Through the night, I questioned myself.
"Why?"

Snowflakes

Soft and white and fun.
I sprinkle the trees
under the frosty sky.
One of many singing stars.
Dark clouds welcome me back
to a snowy day.

The Thin Black Line

The thin black lines on my note pad
leave no shadow.
I fill these lines with characters of black
and feelings of the rainbow.

The blank clock
moves time only when you're enjoying it,
slowing down when you aren't.
Its hands walk across the numbers,
circles and circles,
sometimes slower and sometimes faster.
Time is a racoon,
intelligent and very mysterious,
for time knows why
and where and what and now.

The never-ending blue sky
shields the earth
and leaves us in wonder.
So when we fly,
we find clouds of cotton,
stars of fire,
and the moon of a new world.

The Wind Tucked Me in Last Night

The kiss of moonlight,
lighting my smile.
The hum of the wind,
pulling the blanket over my tired self.
The music of the wind chime,
swaying outside.
The hum of streetlights,
flickering and dancing.
The open window,
letting the wind come and tuck me in.

Bone Moon

A bone moon in a waterfall sky.
A shadow over the waterfall.
The sun shining on the bone.
Scratches big as craters,
pebbles glimmering like stars.
A fish with blue and white fins glides.
The color of aging, yellow,
on this lifeless bone.
I look up to see a lake above me,
and a desert bone floating in the sky.

Glares and Wishes

The light glares at the dark,
shriveling it away.
Only when the light disappears,
the darkness creeps
and darkens the shadows,
warming the room
with the coldness of the dark.

The ocean looked up to the sky,
wishing that it could have a warm sun
comforting the wet coldness.
The sky looked down at the ocean,
wishing that fish could breathe air
and swim in the sky.

Mr. Nobody

Mr. Nobody wants to be somebody,
but he simply can't be seen.
He's the one who startled you last night
by pushing your chair out from the table.
You squinted and wondered
how this could happen,
but later blamed it on the cat.
Mr. Nobody used to be the Invisible Man,
but really, he is just Mr. Nobody.

Wind

Whistle and blow
as you and your rapid
winds topple over any obstacle.
Invisible and invincible,
fighting birds that fly your way.
Never in the history of wind
have you yielded.

It rolls without touching the ground.
It whistles without a mouth,
and it flies without wings.
You can't see it or taste it,
yet you feel it and smell it,
moving fast through the sky,
brushing your hair and giving you a whiff
of what is beyond the horizon.

It sometimes forms hands
and grabs things for itself,
but eventually feels guilty
and sets them down.
Every day, you smell and touch
the wind.

Owl

Graceful wings flap in a disorganized pattern.
Endless words floating through your head
but can't get to your mouth.
Eyes staring without rest
until you blink.
Feathery speckled owls
rain down fluff when they fly.
And that feather
just landed on your windowsill.
Endless horizons
where they disappear.

It's All Inside

Inside a table is the wood
that was carved into a table.
Inside the wood is a redwood tree,
with fingers clenching the dirt below
and strong legs.
Inside a redwood tree
is the shapeless water that hydrated the tree.
Inside water is a sea full of life.
Inside the sea is the sand,
neatly resting at the bottom of the ocean.
Inside sand is a boulder
on the highest mountaintop.
On the boulder is a person climbing.
That person is you.
So you see, there are seas and trees
and rocks and sand,
and even you
inside of each table.

Stellar Jay

The stellar jay wore a beautiful crown,
sapphire blue wings
and midnight black eyes.
Its long and graceful wings
swept through the air,
creating a stir in the autumn
brown and yellow leaves
on the ground far below.

A squawk startled the valley
as the stellar jay
fought over a nut with a russet squirrel.
As the stellar jay flew
back to his lonely nest,
the nut managed to fall
from the sharp beak
and plummeted
to the bottom of the sky.

A graceful bird swept it from the air
just as it fell to the ground,
and as the stellar jay
chased after the nut,
he met eyes with another
stellar jay.

Swallowtail Butterfly

A stained glass window
with a shade of yellow brighter than the sun
and a shade of black darker than midnight.
Yet this art is three-dimensional
and can flutter to the very top
of the white rose,
where the swallowtail butterfly
curled her tongue.
Her thoughts reflect the thoughts of a humble
yet simple-minded human,
but her eyes reflect only the nectar
from the flower where she flew.

Lightning Storm

On and off, in and out,
invisible and visible,
right and wrong.
Lights changing, on or off?
I ask these questions
between blinking lights.
The physical switch doesn't move,
but the room is suddenly dark
for a fraction of a second.
The mental switch wildly flies,
back and forth.

Prophesy

The poem I don't want to write
would be about war and too many secrets.
The birds wouldn't chirp,
and there would be no sweet smell after the rain.
Education would be as lost as the minds of violent people.
Everything and everyone would be screaming in pain.
The game would be called
"Who can start the most unreasonable fight."
This is a poem I don't and won't
and will never write about,
and this is also my worst fear.
But yesterday, the grass told me
it was coming true.

Sunset

A sun setting, never rising again.
A shooting star about to burn out.
The last glimpse of a loved one.
The never in this sentence.
The sun will set forever one day,
so cherish light and warmth,
a loving hand on your shoulder.

Don't wait!
The sun won't need sunglasses
for your baby brother's eyes.
That soldier will fall,
day will be night,
and night will be night.

Darkness, cold, night.

Invisible Ink

An invisible pen with invisible ink
writing the best poem of all.
The paper, soaked with ink,
but whiter than the clouds.
The pen stops moving.
It makes the sighing sound of an old pen.
It hasn't touched the paper.
I ponder this, head tilted, elbows on table,
thoughts tangled like uncombed hair.
Then the pen writes something in visible ink.
That's the best poem of all!

Nightmare

I wake up, heart hammering
against my chest so hard
it feels like it is trying to break
out of my chest.
My mind replays the memory
of my worst nightmare –
a dream shattering any happiness
I could have had that day.
A dream that leaves me lying on the kitchen floor
two stories away from my room.
A dream where war is love
and love is war.
A dream where I am alone.

Dreams of the Dirt

The speechless pile of dirt
dreams of being shoveled
into a pile and walked on.
In the dream, it sprouts legs,
arms and feet and hands,
and a face with of mop
of brown hair.
It has a low, booming voice
filling its empty throat.
And if its throat can be filled
with a voice,
his tongue will say,
"Your turn!"

Sunrise

The waking sun yawns
and releases the scent of colors.
Fog rolls in on mouse feet,
morning dew clinging to the awakened
sharp blades of grass.
A song rises,
chirps and croaks and creeks.
It tastes like sunlight
finally landing on your tongue
after a cold, misty night
of waiting.

Fog

I spread my wings and fly,
so graceful, yet a blur.
Soft eyes that blink,
but when you come
I fly away.

Everything is Connected, Yet Different

A dog is like a cat, yet different.
A cat is like an owl, wise and mysterious.
An owl is like a child, learning more and more.
A child is like a flower, blooming and growing.
A flower is like a blank piece of paper,
waiting for its destiny.
A blank piece of paper is like a puff of inspiration,
waiting to be noticed.
A puff of inspiration is like a skeleton,
supporting what it holds onto.
A skeleton is like you, staying strong each day.
You are like a flame, shining its best
while flickering and dancing away.

Tonight

Close your eyes, so the world goes black.
Turn off your light,
and bring out smaller ones.
Whisper faintly in my ear,
Shhh . . . Shhh . . . Shhh . . .

Let the world fall into a deep sleep,
but wake us later,
while turning the sky back
into a light blue.

When I open my eyes,
I pray that I can
experience you again,
tonight.

Eyes of the Crow

Eyes stare deep enough
to sink into your head,
never glaring,
never smiling,
although sometimes
in the dimmest moonlight,
they flash an impossible look
that sometimes seems soft.

Hobble and Drag

I glide gracefully through the water.
My fast swimming is your walking.
But every once in a while,
I am washed up on the rough sand.
I hobble and drag myself
back off the land.

The One and Only World

The one and only rock
I have in my hand
is wet and it shimmers
as I return it to the water.

The one and only roof
keeps me from the cold,
so that I can quickly escape
by opening the door.

The one and only world
provides us with all of our needs.
You can't get away from the world
without choking on pure, lifeless space.

If There Were No Questions . . .

If there were no questions,
you would walk around without a purpose.
"Wonder," that word I rejoice when I hear it,
wouldn't be a word.
Scientists would lose their jobs
or quit because they know everything
there is to know.
Life would be as blank as a new piece of paper,
except without the enjoyment
of finally putting the first blob of ink
on the page.

The Magical Box

Lined with crystals,
made by fairies,
blessed by the gods,
and loved by all living things.
The box of mystical magic
is the one and only best.

Not for people
younger than three years of age!

A Dream Catcher's Thoughts

Bad dreams, good dreams, weird dreams, sad dreams —
that's all I can think about.
I watch the beautiful good-as-gold dreams
slowly float through my woven net,
and the frightening dreams trying to shoot through.
But I'm fast, so I block the bad dreams
from the child I protect.
I'm high above, hanging and sometimes
rocking back and forth
on my little hook.

Imagination

Suppose you traveled to a faraway land
where the journey is hard.
People sometimes call this place close,
but only if you know how to get there.
Then, it would be so close
that it would literally be right above your eyes.
Very few people have ventured there —
even the people who get short glimpses
of that mysterious land.
But at night, people get longer glimpses.
Most people just think it's their brain,
but a human being can't do
that type of magic.

On the Golden Gate Bridge

The sea floated over and under me,
yet I was standing on dry land.
The wind petted my face,
and my hair tried to escape from my hat.
I found my eyes sleeping,
but my brain was still wide awake.
I touched the blue sky
and ate the clouds.
My breath slowed and relaxed,
and my arms spread out
as I hugged the air.

In Heaven

The smell of cherry blossoms
welcomes guests.
The ground is softer than cotton candy,
more hypnotizing than the clouds.
Water reflects feelings,
and an image showing your inner self,
filling pools and lakes and waterfalls.
Plants would be the same, but our
feelings for them would be different.
Beds would be for everyone
and would be softer than angels' wings
as they hover in the sky.
All of this in heaven,
and hopefully, soon on earth.

Croak Like the Creek

Legs of a frog,
but tail of a tadpole.
Like a butterfly emerging
from its cocoon too soon.
A croak like the creak
of an old oak.
Stripes of the t-shirt
it wears day and night,
sleeping and in flight.
It jumps at the speed of light.
Eyes on both sides
watching, watching lights —
and the firefly it chews
tonight.

The Dragon Soars

A stained glass door
opening and closing.
The dragon soars
to a place unknown,
unknown to man and dragon,
past the horizon.

A Bit of Black Paint

I accidently elbowed
over the black paint,
and the universe filled with color.
Books can't choose a color,
flashing bright pinks and dull grays.
Trees are purple,
      tables are yellow,
            chairs are green
and I am myself.
It's amazing how colorful the world can get
with a bit of paint.

Waiting

Waiting for land to come.
Waiting for another chance at life.
Waiting for a greeting from the sun.
Waiting for a dreadful feeling
that pulls at you.
It feels like a simple, painful wait.
A weight on life.

Red Boots

Neatly on their own shelf,
reflecting a bright light,
imagining the muddy world outside
and how they would splash in the deepest puddles.
Their thirst for both adventure and water
took over their red shininess,
but soon two hands grabbed them.
When they were returned to the shelf,
they were wet, muddy and happy.

Snow

Warming the childlike earth
A white blanket falls
upon heads of all people.
The snow warms the dirt.

Drifting Boats

Windows opening,
closing, also reflecting.

A picture that's framed,
glimpses of an unknown world.

Outside, it's raining,
foggy and dark.

Prisoner

Invisible bars and walls of glass,
a small, invisible prison.
A shocked face, frozen in time
moves hands across the long
walls of the prison.

Enchanted Cats

Fifty eyes staring.
The eyes belong to slim bodies.
Whiskers pointing straight out,
a fur coat of magic.
Like a hermit crab's shell,
unpredictable but beautiful.

Their shadows dance with excitement and wonder,
but their eyes send curious glances at me.
Their tails don't twitch.
A soft dream,
with circles and triangles and diamonds
framing a silent face.

One tail flinches, and the eyes
send sharp daggers at the tail.
When the eyes are on top of me again,
my fingers creep under a chin
and scratch it.

My dreams light up
in a thousand colors.
Enchanted eyes,
beautiful sweater of fur.

In the Nowhere of the Ocean

A seed drops onto the ground.
It is lifted and flies
wildly gliding toward black water,
thrashed back and forth by waves.
It settles on the sandy ground,
as a long storm finally ends.
Soon, the seed is moving
at lightning-fast speed,
too fast for the human eye to see.
One hundred years later, there is no seed.
Instead, a tall willow tree,
standing in the nowhere of the ocean.

Fog, mist and a dark sky greet me.
It tickles my nose
as if I am the only thing it touched.
Water surrounds me,
but I can see the island shimmering
like a tiny star on the horizon.

It isn't only me here —
I'm rocking with the waves,
and the mist,
although nothing seems alive or moving.
I know that everything is stirring.
The ocean breeze carries salt
that makes my eyes squint.
A shadow casts over me.

My awkward movements somehow
get me turned around.
A long, wide creature stares down at me
with old eyes.
Its arms hug me.
The willow tree is beautiful,
swaying in the nowhere of the ocean.

The Hugging Fog

Feathers of thin fog
slowly sing a lullaby
that awakens instead of tucks
beings into a sound sleep.
Fog hugs the gentle grass
and weaves the most beautiful dreams.
A sight of wonder —
one that will hug you
instead of haunt you.

The Nothing

The nothing turned into a something.
The ink turned into a pen.
The earth turned into a snowball.
The zebra turned into a sad song.
The gun turned into a bouquet.
The bowl turned into a present.
The future turned into the past.
The past turned invisible, waiting endlessly.

The Mysterious Room

The world is a trance
of reds and pinks
jumping out at you,
mirrors reflecting your amazed face.

The floor collapses
like bending origami paper,
but your mouth is still
spread out on your face.

The sky dances
and can't make up its mind.
A beautiful trap
that takes you on a ride,
forever.

Dancing in the Moonlight

My own disco ball
spins without electricity
at the highest speeds.
It is old and big
and plays the best songs
of adventure and curious aliens.
The mist will bead
like plump pearls on my forehead
as I dance like fire,
refusing to be put out.
The fog will make intruders
look at me mysteriously
with a scared look that I love.
My naked feet will jump high
and create a stir in the blankets
of heavy, cold fog.
I will be blinded by reality,
living the new reality
of dancing in the moonlight.

My Desk

A box of something,
everything and nothing,
my messy desk opens.
The pencils and pens
don't fit into the small jar,
but they never did.
The trinkets and toys
play without thought or reason,
spilled across my desk.

I Open My Eyes

I open my eyes and see the striking earth
that we call our world.
I see that night has set,
and only the smallest feather of fog stirs.

I close my eyes and sleep.
With a pillow of clouds under my head,
I am greeted by my friends in their dreams.

I open my eyes to our astounding planet's sun
and see the light it gives to those who don't see.

I close my eyes and see nothing.
I open my eyes, then blink.

Fire

Fire
unknown and mysterious
stretching to the sun,
fighting the breath's fingers.
Consuming the wick,
scaring the wax
down
to the bottom.
An acquaintance with smoke,
who loves warmth.

A Planet is Like a Dizzy Child

A planet is like a dizzy child.
A dizzy child is like a tall, old tree.
A tall old tree is like a castle in the mist.
A castle in the mist is like a young parrot
with awkward movements.
A young parrot with awkward movements
is like an eye reflecting the unknown.
An eye reflecting the unknown is like a light bulb,
just turned on.
A light bulb, just turned on is like a dizzy child.
A dizzy child is like a planet.

Six Word Stories

1. Kai, the kicking Karate Kid, kicked.
2. Pink polka-dotted parrots pecking peas.
3. Pearl's pen wondered yonder to ponder.

My Own Way

I moved the sun and bought a new, warm planet
to act as earth's heater.
The new sun was too hot,
so I moved a table to the sky
to shade hot people.
Turns out, gravity hated floating things,
so it wrecked a house.
I stopped paying the gravity bills
so everyone could float,
but no one liked it.
People and birds floated into space.
I detached houses from the ground,
and brought the ground to them.
Everyone went into their houses
and floated into space.
Now I have my own planet
of chaos.

Hatred of Poems

Without fiery music in the soul,
they live a plain, thoughtless life.
Mental pictures of great triumphs:
pouring cereal, lifting a mug, blinking.
A rather pointless life.

They won't know what it feels like
to be lifted into the air
in your own thoughts,
flying,
flying.

And back on the floor,
ready to show your teacher
the great work you've done.

It's a choice that you make.
Fly, or fall asleep in boredom.

The Secret of the Smile

The secret of the smile
is that lips are the curtains,
always ready to frame some teeth,
and actors are good at acting.
The secret of the butterfly
is that she was once a flower
whose petals thinned into wings.
The secret of the skeleton
is that science
shouldn't have anything to do with you.
The secret of the child
is that those new eyes
see through you.
The secret of the book
is that is really does have a voice.

Four Seasons

1. Fall

Colors of caramel,
burnt but with a sweet smell.
Leaves slowly snail their way down.
The autumn breeze collects them
into neat piles.
They'll swallow you if you jump inside,
and cling to your hair
through the whole day.
The sun is a ripe tangerine
steadily standing in the sky.
Rolling clouds like cottony hills.

2. Winter

A fire of white
burning everything in its sight,
garnishing the naked trees
with a colorful charcoal.
Untouched, animals hide away
deep in the ground,
sleeping a soundless sleep
until the fire melts.
Dancing winds are playing with the cold,
which is hugging the quiet world.

3. Spring

Flowers and trees with green jackets
color the sunny ground.
Floral, sweet and happy,
drifting from the wafting air
onto our tongues.
Sharp but soft blades of grass
hold backpacks of morning dew.
Sugar is swallowed by the clouds,
pink in an orange sky.

4. Summer

Sun slaps against sweaty backs.
Water in large puddles swish,
wherever you go.
Sunglasses on heads, flip-flops on feet.
Female birds in bright colors
sit on nests, hoping
to add a new bird to the family.
Male birds rush back and forth,
feeding their mate most of their food.
A happy chatter floating in the air.
Smiles fill faces,
the ones performing jumping jacks in pure bliss.

The Pen Colors Me

As I write a song,
beautiful music dances in front of me.
The pen colors me.
It shapes my world
and splashes color
in the darkest of shadows.
Colors that are vibrant and living.
It makes me clear my eyes
so that I can admire
the work that others have done.
The pen makes a mouth
so that I can be speechless at the world.
But mostly, the pen gives me these presents
so that I can see the light
in the darkness,
so that I can see who others
really are,
and what makes the shadows
brighter for them.

Cloud Ripping

The quiet trees whisper goodnight.
The wind sweeps the song
across the land.
A hushed hill
nestles a rock ledge
where a wolf once stood.
She dares not stand alone,
or where would her cubs sleep?
One cuddles, one pleads for play.
One tears apart the clouds
with a simple howl.
That howl
wasn't a howl of pain
or sorrow,
but a howl of something
enchanting, magical, wondrous,
and cloud-ripping.

Silence

Fingers of light caress the jackets,
crying on the hangers
in the slim hallway,
soon to retreat completely
off the horizon
at the sun's demand.

The soft, muffled yapping
of the cars on the streets
toll in my ear,
the little sound
that makes the trip home.

I stroke the small words
on the back of the spoon
in my hand.
They make the largest ridges.

I glance at a feather
from my molting, loud bird
that the housecleaner missed
and the vacuum cleaner forgot
on the floor.
It displays a green
at the base of the feather
and blends slowly and evenly
into a bottomless, otherworldly blue.

A silence holds the air
as I stand smacking myself
in my thoughts
because the feather doesn't respond.

Why, feather?
Why can't I be perfect like you?

The Cat Lady's Grey Backyard

The ground is a bongo drum.
The peaks of the rooftops
of San Francisco
are hugging the dirt
and shielding it.
The waves blow a tune
onto faraway wind chimes
that are now swaying
in the cat lady's grey backyard.
The fire flickers
off and on.
The sky's hand pounds,
echos wind chimes.
A beautiful song plays
while the fox huddles in her burrow
because the bongo drum plays
so hard that outside
it begins to rain.

The Fox's Stare

What emotions does your face hold?
With your eyes glistening
in the cold early morning sun,
they reflect my awed expression.
Your tail holds mischief.
You hold it high
so it can feel the breeze
twisting away from the clouds.

Why don't you cry
on the nights when you're alone?
The wolves have their howl;
the doves have their sad coos.
How do you let out
the feelings you shoo?

The fox just stares
with her starry eyes
because even when the moon
seems to cry,
and the nights extend
to reveal their dark, pitiful lies,
the fox never cries.

Untouched

The trail that leads
out of town
has hardly any human footprints found.
The ivy adorns
a young sapling's arms.
Spring blossoms peel open,
revealing an acrylic masterpiece.
But why it is untouched,
I still ponder,
for the road that leads yonder
is so beautiful.
Perhaps it is all eye's music
because it is untouched.

Wet Trail

My closed eye's raindrops
plummet to the ground,
leaving a wet trail of sadness
soon to be found.
But no one will be astounded,
for my eyes
are often wounded,
tightly closed.

Where is the World Coming To?

A shadow consumes the edge of town.
Smog darkens the clouds.
The buildings grow higher;
oil fields grow wider.
The flower tucked into mother's hair
is wilted with age.
The last tree
stands with rage,
and a crow with an important message
never delivers the page,
for the shadow that is us
has no cage.

About the Author

Pearl Werbach is an eleven-year-old poet who attends the Brandeis School of San Francisco. She was awarded second place in the Northern California Immigration Council writing contest in 2017. When she is not writing poetry, she is with her quirky bird, a Sun Conure named Mango.

www.ingramcontent.com/pod-product-compliance
Lightning Source LLC
Chambersburg PA
CBHW032027090426
42741CB00006B/751